THE BEST FRIENDS'

Guide to

Bedroom

Decorating

SCHOLASTIC INC.

New York   Toronto   London   Auckland   Sydney
Mexico City   New Delhi   Hong Kong   Buenos Aires

ISBN 0-439-68946-5

Text copyright © 2003 by Gill Sutherland
Illustrations copyright © 2003 by Kirstie Aitken

12 11 10 9 8 7 6 5 4 3   4 5 6 7 8 9/0

Printed in the U.S.A.   40

First printing, October 2004

Contents

Want to be Friends?   **5**
The part where you get to meet Molly and your
new Best Friends

Let the makeover begin!   **11**
Dealing with parents; deciding on what
you're going to do with your bedroom and how
to get organized — but in a good *fun* way, honest!

Themes, schemes, and blueprints   **25**
How to start thinking creatively about your room

Ultimate bedroom makeovers   **41**
What's YOUR ideal color scheme? Which theme
is for YOU? Decide right here as we show you six
of the coolest dream bedrooms ever created

Making the most of what you've got 59

Making your junk funky; creating moods;
necessary accessories; and changing a wild
mess into a neat nest!

Stuff to make 79

We're talking secret-stash stowaway cushions,
funky four-poster beds (yes, you, too, can have
one!), mesmerizing murals, and a ton of other
show-off projects

Your bedroom-decorating problems solved 97

From the most annoying, room-sharing
little sis in the world to the most boring bedroom
in Snoozeville — we take your problems and get
them solved

The quiz 104

R U a bedroom beauty or a bedroom bozo?
Dare ya to find out!

Other room makeovers 116

From sci-fi to 1950s retro — they're all here!

⭐ Want to be Friends? ⭐

The name's Molly, Molly White. (I know, a bit dull — I'm currently thinking up an exotic middle name. Got any ideas?) It's great to meet you and I can tell we're going to get along just fine!

Me and my friends, Flower, Bubble, Missy, and Princess (aka the Best Friends), love thinking up ways we can improve the everyday lives of "girlkind" throughout this planet we call "Earth." (Why we gave our own part of the universe such a boring name and wasted brilliant names like "Venus" on other parts is beyond me.) But, anyway, to get back to what I was saying, if you're looking for top-quality advice sprinkled with the occasional joke, then look no further than right here! It is our mission to serve you, O Earth maiden!

Before I introduce you to the rest of the Best Friends, here's a little more about me:

Full name: Molly _____ (insert exciting middle-name suggestion here) White

Distinguishing features: Dazzling beauty and huge brain! (OK, I've got brown spiky hair, I'm kind of short, and my teachers figure I've got "potential"!)

5

Family history: One male parent (Dad), one female parent (Mom), and one incredibly annoying twin brother (Billy = bothersome boy). And we live in a boring town I call Dullsville.

Life would be totally dull without: Long words, chocolate, poems, most music, and hanging out in my bedroom with my Best Friends.

Pet peeves: Mean people, pollution, Brussels sprouts (one question: why?), and uninvited snoopers coming into my bedroom (especially ones called Billy).

Current bedroom decor: Relaxed vibes (OK, it's really messy), walls painted deep, dark purple and midnight blue, with gold stars on the ceiling, bulging bookcases, and lots of big velvet cushions.

Over to you now, Best Friends — tell our new Friend all about yourselves!

Flower

AKA: Flower Spirit Delaney (Molly: "Now, *that's* what I call a groovy middle name!")

Life would be totally dull without: "Nature! I adore all animals and wildlife. And I'm really into feng shui and other new-age stuff."

Pet peeves: "Cruelty to animals, and bullying."

Fave bedroom feature: "My canopy bed!"

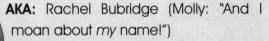

Bubble

AKA: Rachel Bubridge (Molly: "And I moan about *my* name!")

Life would be totally dull without: "Having fun with the BFs, shouting, running (I'm the best runner in my school — boast!), eating pizzas, and really, really loud music."

Pet peeves: "People who make fun of others — and, well, having to share a bedroom with my little sister."

Fave bedroom feature: "The collage of photos me and the BFs have made over the years!"

7

AKA: Nora Baxter (Molly: "We only call her Missy, though!")

Life would be totally dull without: "My cell phone, my computer, R&B and jazz, cool clothes, and gossip!"

Pet peeves: "Untidiness and snobs — oh, and a low battery!"

Fave bedroom feature: "My funky orange and black color scheme!"

AKA: Pandora Elizabeth Alexandra Moxbury (Molly: "How many classy names can one girl have, eh?!")

Life would be totally dull without: "Shopping, art, painting, and glossy magazines."

Pet peeves: "Having no money, and stuck-up people."

Fave bedroom feature: "'The Salon' — well, that's what we Friends call it — it's just my makeup table, really, but it's crammed with beauty products, and it's where we spend hours doing makeovers!"

So your room needs a makeover, huh? Luckily you've come to the right place. This book is bursting with the best makeover tips and latest gorgeous looks for cool bedrooms. Read on and we'll show you how to:

★ Ask your parents for their permission and help!
★ Turn a dull room into a dazzling dream-palace!
★ Free your inner artist and become a sensational style queen!

All those in favor of joining the Best Friends on their adventure into bedroom-makeovers, turn the page now!

Welcome, Friend! Now, since you're officially one of us, it's my pleasure to offer you our sacred pledge:

The Best Friends' pledge

1. To be on hand with our expert advice 24/7, sleeping by your side if necessary.

   ★

2. To never give up on you — even if you completely ignore our advice.

   ★

3. To never hardly ever laugh at your mistakes, off-the-wall fads, and truly crazy ideas.

   ★

4. Basically, you have our undying love, loyalty blah blah blah, and can borrow any of our things, anytime...for eternity!

Hmm. With a touch of gold paint, that pledge would look lovely hung above your bed. Oh, listen to me, I've started already! That must mean it's time for our first chapter....

Let the Makeover Begin!

66 First off, let's take a moment to really love our bedrooms! 99

66 Uh-oh! Flower's having one of her hippie-dippy moments! 99

66 No, seriously! My mom, who I admit is kind of a hippie, told me before I redecorated my room that I had to really think about what I used my 'space' for and to really appreciate it. That way I would know what style it should have. 99

That sounds reasonable. I love my room because it's where my beloved bed is, and I do like my ZZZZs! Friends, why do you love your bedrooms?

"I can do my own thing without being spied on!**"**

"Because it's where I go to think about things.**"**

"It's where I keep all my stuff.**"**

"It's where me and the Friends chill.**"**

" OK, so bedrooms are great! Now grab the glitter paint, and let's decorate! **"**

Hmm, nice rapping, Bubble, but before our Friend starts painting, she's got to answer three very important little questions, which we'll call:

The BFs' pre-makeover triple challenge!

OK, so I've given this part a fancy title to disguise the fact that this is where you have to think sensibly about three key things before you begin your bedroom makeover.

WATCH IT, Friend!

We must warn you that failure to think about these three practical considerations will mean you'll be destined to live forever in a pit of disorganized chaos, with zero style and really lame furniture chosen by your mom when you were, like, five!

Sensible thought 1: How can I get my parents' permission?

66 Oh, I can help with this part! I've become kind of an expert in the field of parent persuading, having had many years practicing on my own mom and dad! 99

66 Tell 'em about the Persuaders, P! 99

66 Ah, yes, The Persuaders are arguments we BFs use to try to convince our parents to let us do our projects. Let me demonstrate....You will note that I've made two kinds of points. The average parent usually is convinced after the mini point, but if not, you'll need to use the major point to try making your case. Look out for more Persuaders as we go! 99

Princess's Parent Persuader No. 1

YOU WANT: to make over your bedroom.

THE PARENTS WANT: you to leave things as they are.

TYPICAL PARENT QUOTE: "But your room's very pretty as it is and, anyway, I thought you liked fluffy bunny rabbits."

MINI POINT: Show them not only that your tastes have changed since your room was last done (circa a gazillion years ago) but also that you are sensible and responsible, by bagging up all the things in your room that you've grown out of – old dolls, clothes, etc. – and telling your parents you'd like to give your stuff to the local thrift store. Finally, win them over by showing them your super-organized plans for your bedroom makeover.

MAJOR POINT: Make a promise that if you are allowed to make over your room, you will keep it neat forever – moms especially like this offer. You might also mention that a new-look bedroom would probably inspire greater homework productivity.

Nice case, Princess! Once you've got The Parents' permission for an all-out bedroom makeover, the next thing to do is to plan your budget and schedule.

"Yawnsville!"

"Don't listen, Friend! Bubble tried to skip this part when she was redoing her room, and she ended up having to paint her walls *after* her new shelves had been put up — she got paint everywhere! And then she blew her budget on take-out pizza for us Friends, which meant she never got her room finished!"

"I'm gonna get around to it soon, no probs!"

Yeah, right! The choice is yours, Friend. Do you want to be a Do-It-Over Bubble or a Super-solver?

Right, all of you wannabe Super-solvers, grab your wallets and prepare to count those precious pennies!

Sensible thought 2: How much money do I have?

Once you've counted up your pennies (yes, even the sticky fuzzy ones from the back of the sofa) and figured out how much money you've got, it's time to start thinking about what you can actually afford to do with it. If your penny pile is kind of pathetic, go for a few trendy touches here and there rather than an all-out makeover — and don't worry. Whatever your budget, we Friends have thought of loads of tips for jazzing up your space!

Before you begin redecorating, you should try to get an idea of how much things cost — check out prices in magazines and catalogs as well as stores. If something you want turns out to be mega expensive, come up with a cheaper idea.

66What if our Friend has no pennies, not even sticky fuzzy ones?!**99**

Try asking your parents to make a cash donation to your worthy cause....

Princess's Parent Persuader No. 2

YOU WANT: cash for your awesome new bedroom makeover.

THE PARENTS WANT: to spend no more than two pennies (or thereabouts).

TYPICAL PARENT QUOTE: "You seem to think we're made of money!" or "It doesn't grow on trees, y'know!"

MINI POINT: Explain that you plan to redo your room really cheaply, and you've hunted for the best bargains in town. Then present your modest budget calculations – how could they fail to recognize what a sensible young lady you are?!

MAJOR POINT: Show your commitment with constant money-making schemes (polishing Dad's shoes, walking the dog, etc.). It's hard not to help someone who's helping herself. Your parents may be so impressed they'll help finance your project.

Best Friends TOP TIP

Even if a cash crisis means that your budget is exactly zilch, don't worry. It's amazing how you can transform your bedroom by something as simple as rearranging the furniture or jazzing up your old junk (see Bubble's tips on page 72).

★

❝Well, that covers the cash and The Parents. We're ready to redecorate!!!**❞**

★

Hold your horses, Bubs! We haven't covered the thing you always run out of . . . time!

Sensible thought 3: How much time do I have?

It's important to set aside a realistic amount of time to complete your makeover. You won't want to rush things, but you also don't want things to drag on and on or be in danger of being dropped because you got bored with it! A weekend seems a reasonable amount of time for a good re-do. Also make sure you schedule it for a time when you won't have homework to do — e.g., during school breaks — and when a parent can be around, in case you need their help.

Once you've figured out when you're going to do your makeover, the next step is to work out what order you should do things in and how long it's going to take to finish each job.

66 The best advice I've ever got from my 'do-it-yourself expert' father is that you should estimate how long each task will take — then double it! 99

Hey, Flower, to show our Friend an example of how she could schedule her project — could you dig out the plans we Friends made when we helped with your two-day bedroom makeover?!"

66 Oh, you mean the Super-solver Schedule! Good idea. I'd have been lost without it! First of all, though, our Friend should know the seven steps I took to turn my dull, cutesy bedroom into a sophisticated hangout for a happening chick (that's me!) and her cool girlfriends! Here's my original 'To Do' list: 99

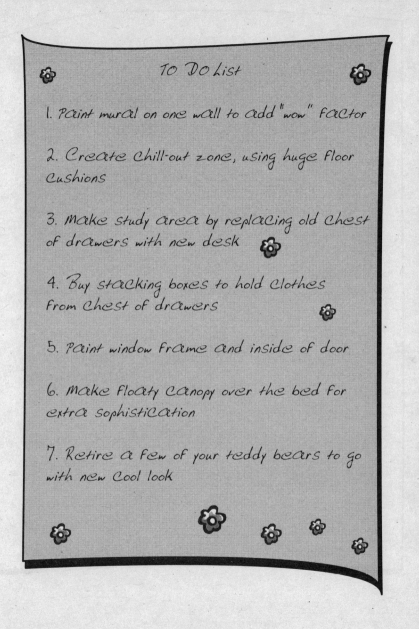

TO DO List

1. Paint mural on one wall to add "wow" factor

2. Create chill-out zone, using huge floor cushions

3. Make study area by replacing old chest of drawers with new desk

4. Buy stacking boxes to hold clothes from chest of drawers

5. Paint window frame and inside of door

6. Make floaty canopy over the bed for extra sophistication

7. Retire a few of your teddy bears to go with new cool look

Flower's Super-Solver Schedule

Time	Task ★
Day 1: 10 a.m.	General preparation: Clear away all clutter Protect all surfaces with old sheets ★
11 a.m.	Painting: Draw mural outline Prepare window and door frames for painting — then paint on first coat
1 p.m.	Lunch break
2 p.m.	Start painting mural ★
4 p.m.	Make floor cushions
Day 2: 10 a.m.	More painting: Do second coat (if necessary) on window and door frames Finish painting mural

I chose a weekend to complete my bedroom makeover, with an extra day the weekend before to buy all the stuff I needed and to have the chest of drawers removed and desk delivered. Here's my timetable. As we went along, I checked off all the jobs one by one.

1 p.m.	Lunch break
2 p.m.	Make canopy above bed
4 p.m.	Rearrange and tidy up: Remove old sheets Arrange floor cushions for more seating Create study area on new desk Store some teddy bears away (sob!)
5 p.m.	Ta-daa! Be amazed at sight of "new" bedroom!

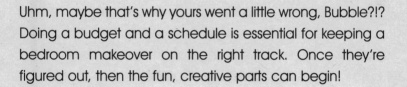

"Man, you were so organized! I remember you even had a clipboard — serious or what?!? I never had anything like that when I did my room!"

Uhm, maybe that's why yours went a little wrong, Bubble?!? Doing a budget and a schedule is essential for keeping a bedroom makeover on the right track. Once they're figured out, then the fun, creative parts can begin!

"Yippee! I love the artsy-crafty jobs!"

Themes, Schemes, and BluePrints

We hope you've got those creative brain juices flowing, Friend, because in this chapter we are going to help you:

★ Identify your own very special style
★ Learn some neat stuff about color
★ Plan a design for your fabulous new *boudoir* (fancy French for dreamy fem bedroom!)

Let's start with the "style" thing. . . .

Whether you're planning a total new look for your bedroom or just a few touches here and there, you'll want it done in a style that fits your tastes and says something about gorgeous little old YOU!

❝And just how do you know what your 'style' is?!❞

25

Simple! Make a storyboard!

❝I saw a designer on TV do one of these, but he called his a 'mood-maker'!**❞**

Call it what you want, but a storyboard is basically a big piece of cardboard filled with loads of pictures that you can use as inspiration for redecorating your room. Here's how to make one:

How to make your very own style-detecting storyboard
First get the following:
★ A big piece of cardboard ★ As many magazines, brochures, and catalogs as you can find (Don't take your mom's without asking, though!) ★ Glue ★ Scissors

Next: Flip through the magazines, cutting out any pictures you like. They can be pictures of rooms, people, places, objects, or even just colors. The important thing is that they should all reflect your tastes.

For example, you could choose pictures of cool people with styles you admire, groovy pieces of furniture you like, or even a T-shirt you like the color of.

Then: Stick all your cutouts onto your cardboard — placing them either randomly to make one big collage or into sections, with one area for your favorite colors, one for fabulous furniture, etc.

Finally: Use your finished storyboard to inspire your fabulous new bedroom. For example, if your storyboard is full of pinks and pictures of sparkly objects, maybe a pink palace of girly loveliness is the bedroom for you! Or if you've chosen lots of shots of glamorous  movie stars and stylish homes for your storyboard, then a sophisticated room with bold colors and lots of luxurious, velvety fabrics is maybe your kind of thing.

But before you go wild with the glitter or velvet, Missy thought of four very handy rules to make sure you've picked the theme that's really right for you.

Missy's four rules for picking a theme:

Rule 1 Go for something that suits your personality; if you're a couch potato, a sports theme won't do!

Rule 2 Get inspired by your own stuff — e.g., if you collect alien-themed stuff, consider a futuristic look.

Rule 3 Don't be a slave to one theme — if your storyboard has more than one, think about how you can make them all work together!

Rule 4 Imagine how your chosen look will be to live with (Day-Glo orange walls can turn a fun friend into a grumpy grouch on sunny early mornings!) and whether it'll look dated too soon.

Once you decide on a theme that's right for you, the next step is to decide on a color scheme. Your storyboard will contain colors that you love, but Flower's here to make doubly sure you're making the right choices, with her handy guide to the world of color.

What hue are you?

> **❝**Colors are like people. They have personalities of their own and can instantly change the mood of your room. So before you pick your color scheme, make sure it's right for you and your space.**❞**

WARM COLORS

Warm, deep colors like red, red-purple, orange, and yellow give rooms a cozy feel.

Red

Good points: brings excitement, drama, and life; makes bigger rooms inviting

Bad vibe: makes small rooms seem smaller and stuffy

Goes well with: green and gold

People who like red are: enthusiastic, curious, and very bold

Yellow

Good points: sunny and cheerful; brightens dull rooms, making them seem larger, and is creatively stimulating
Bad vibe: not very peaceful
Goes well with: purples
People who like yellow are: bubbly, warm, good at talking and making others laugh, and sporty

Orange

Good points: bold, lively, and fun; encourages conversation and eating!
Bad vibe: not very restful
Goes well with: blue
People who like orange are: charming, attention-seeking but very kindhearted

Pink

Good points: uplifting, soothing, and welcoming
Bad vibes: can look a little cutesy
Goes well with: pale green or lilac
People who like pink are: very affectionate, gentle, and everyone's friend

Princess's Parent Persuader No. 3

YOU WANT: wild and wacky colors.

THE PARENTS WANT: boring and dull or no changes at all.

TYPICAL PARENT QUOTE: "Pink is so unpractical; oatmeal will look lovely, you'll see."

MINI POINT: Agree that you can live with plain walls, but ask for your choice of paint for the woodwork.

MAJOR POINT: Get your parents' opinion: "If you were me, what color scheme would you have, pink or purple?" Have them really think about what would be fun and cool, not just practical. They may end up agreeing with you!

COOL COLORS

Lighter, cooler shades like green, blue, blue-purple, and white give rooms a spacious, elegant feel; so they're especially good if you want your small room to look bigger.

Blue

Good points: symbolizes loyalty and brings harmony, peace, and comfort
Bad vibe: can seem cold
Goes well with: orange
People who like blue are: honest, confident, and good listeners

Green

Good points: the color of nature — it's refreshing and promotes spiritual awareness (or so my hippie mom says!)
Bad vibes: darker shades can be dull
Goes well with: red
People who like green are: mothering types who like to make sure everyone (including themselves) feels fine physically and emotionally

Purple

Good points: strong, powerful, and thought-provoking
Bad vibes: somewhat intense
Goes well with: yellow
People who like purple are: very independent, sensitive, and just a little secretive

Beginning to plan your new bedroom

So, you've chosen your theme and your colors, so it's almost time to put pencil to paper. But hold it right there — before you begin, there are still a few important things to keep in mind.

Even if you've only got a small room, you can make the most of the space by "zoning"....

" Sounds more like something you do to a parking lot than a bedroom! **"**

Ahem. I'll have you know that creating "zones" in your bedroom will not only make it look really cool, it will help you get super organized! All you do is start by thinking about all the things you do in your room: sleep, relax, entertain, dress, make yourself beautiful, etc.

Each activity should have its own place — its "zone" — in your room where you can keep all the supplies and furniture you need for doing it. For example, Princess has created "The Salon" in her room where we do our beauty makeovers. It's centered on her makeup table and chair, where she keeps all her hair products, makeup, and grooming accessories. Almost everything in The Salon is pink!

Don't worry if your room is small — just give one zone two functions! For example, my gossiping zone (four floor cushions plunked on the floor by the door) is also my dressing-up zone. (It's by my clothes closet, the door has a full-length mirror on the back, and there's plenty of room for posing in front of the mirror when I stuff the cushions under the bed.)

Rearranging your furniture is a great way to create zones. For example, moving your bed into the middle of the room (if it's big enough) will give you zones on either side of the bed.

66And then the bed can be your focal point. According to the fancy home-improvement magazines my mom reads, all the best-designed rooms have focal points, or FPs. This is when you emphasize a key feature in your room, so when someone walks in they immediately look at the FP and go, 'Wowweeee!' You can make fab FPs by painting a huge mural, putting string lights around your window, or piling your bed high with fluffy cushions — just use your imagination!99

OK, so how are you visualizing your new room? Is it a swanky, palacelike pad filled with expensive stuff and a luxury bed the size of a football field? Yeah? Uh-oh, Friend, it sounds like you need to get real about what you can actually do with your modest little bedroom. We're talking about facing up to some basic practical considerations. Start by taking this short quiz:

The "have you gone a little bedroom-makeover nuts?" test

Honest answers only, please.

1 Is your bedroom big enough for your fabulous re-do?

2 Have you included essential stuff like your bed, desk, and chest of drawers in your plans?

3 Is there enough money in Mr. Piggy to cover your costs?

4 Are you still going to be able to comfortably sleep, get dressed, do your homework, have friends around, and just chill in your new room?

If you answered a happy yes to all of the above, you may go on to the next step! Anyone who muttered a sulky no will have to sit in a corner until your brain calms down and comes up with something less unrealistic.

The next step

OK, Friend, let's get ready to put all your "braintastic" thoughts into action — yes, it's blueprint time! But don't worry, you don't have to be an artistic genius. As long as you can use a pencil and ruler, you'll be fine! The idea of making a blueprint is to help you get organized, making sure you've thought of everything you'll need for your new room, and to give you a rough idea of what the end result is going to look like. It's not a drawing competition!

❝I love this part — it's where you get to be really arty making groovy illustrations of how your new room's going to look — just like one of those professional designers on TV!**❞**

How to make your blueprint
What you need:

★ A few sheets of graph paper ★Measuring tape ★ Ruler ★ Pencil and eraser (even those pros make constant revisions!) ★ Colored pens or cardboard ★Frilly shirt (ha! not really — unless you actually *want* to look like a super pretend designer, that is!)

What you do:

1 Measure your bedroom — don't forget to do all the walls, windows, and doorways.

2 Also measure larger items like your bed, desk, and chest of drawers.

3 Start plotting the layout and contents of your new room on the paper. Make sure you draw your bedroom to scale. To draw something to scale, try making 2 inches (5 cm) in your drawing represent 36 inches (1 m) in real life. You can change this figure to make your drawing bigger or smaller.

4 Using colored pens or, even better, those paint chips you get free at paint stores, show what colors you plan to use where. You don't need to go crazy coloring in. Just use paint chips or draw small colored squares and put them to the side of your blueprint. Then use arrows or numbers to indicate where each color will go.

To give you an idea of what your blueprint could look like, take a peek at the one we did when we were planning how to redecorate Flower's room.

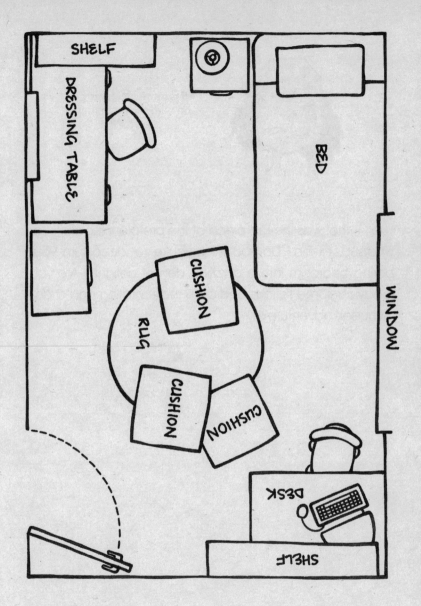

"Can we pleeeeeze get on with the decorating now?!"

Yup — that was the last piece of the pre-planning stuff! So, whatsup, Friend? Do you think you're ready to turn your boring bedroom into a dazzling den of delight?! Are you ready for some serious bedroom redecorating and a do-it-yourself adventure?!?

Ultimate Bedroom Makeovers

I know there will be some of you out there who are grumbling, "Create a dream bedroom out of my tiny shoe box?! Impossible!"

Well, listen up, grumblers, because we BFs have spent hours, days, and sometimes even whole math lessons thinking about this, and we've come up with some easy-to-follow guides to help you create your dream room! Exciting, huh?

Before you know it, your bedroom will be admired by friends, relatives, neighbors, and the worlds of fashion, music, and TV. Don't be surprised if Hollywood calls asking to film the story of your bedroom's creation! Ha!

Three dream bedrooms for dream girls

Molly's mmm—mocha!

Have you noticed just how many coffee bars there are now?!? (Answer: Lots!) I love the ones with the saggy sofas, dim, mood lighting, and deep dark red walls. They look like such a neat place to hang out — either by yourself reading or chillin' with friends. Anyway, that's what inspired this look.

Theme: Coffee-shop chic

Best for: Large rooms

Would appeal to: Deep-thinking, sophisticated Friends who love to read or have brainy conversations with their pals.

Color scheme: Rich burgundy walls, and chocolate brown woodwork.

Special effects: Use gold metallic felt-tip pens to draw loads of hearts and stars — or whatever you want — all around the walls. (It looks arty and breaks up the heaviness of the dark colors.)

Luxury feature/focal point: The "Zen Zone" — special zone designed for entertaining your friends or for moments of quiet thinking! To create the ZZ, get a small, low coffee table (an upturned orange crate or sturdy box with a fancy covering will do!) and surround it with floor cushions. (See page 79 for how to make cushions.)

Added extras: Interesting reading material laid out on coffee table (like this book!) and rich aromas, using coffee-scented candles or incense. (Note the "Watch it, Friend" on page 47.)

(See page 79 for how to make cushions.)

★ Decorating tips ★
Awesome things to do with walls
★ Paint each wall a different color — it'll make your room look bigger and more interesting.
★ Draw out features like radiator covers and window seats by painting them in a contrasting color to the rest of your room.
★ You can get some beautiful wrapping-paper designs; find one you like and cover one wall or area with it, using Sticky Tac to put it up — ta-daa, instant groovy wallpaper!
★ Let your room express your personality by displaying artwork you've made yourself — be proud, you artistic genius, you!
★ Turn one wall into a "photo gallery" — visitors will love teasing you about your "cute" baby photos!

Princess and her chamber of magic!

❝Here, I've been inspired by all things magical and spooky, with a helping hand from some leftover Halloween-party stuff.**❞**

Theme: Old World magic chic

Best for: Medium-sized or attic rooms

Would appeal to: Sensitive, independent-minded Friends with a strong sense of drama!

Color scheme: Paint your walls purple (very mystical looking) unless your room is small. If it is, then think about painting one or two of the other walls in a lighter color — like goldish yellow — to keep the room from feeling too stuffy. Then, to give it that gothic castle touch, paint woodwork, doors, etc., in dark gray or black gloss paint.

Special effects: Along the top of your walls, paint a frieze of the cycle of the moon, using luminous white or glow-in-the-dark paint. Go gradually from new moon to full moon — using about eight "moons" for each cycle. Repeat until you come around to where you started.

You can paint your moons any size, but about 12 inches (30 cm) in diameter is a nice, eye-catching size.

○ ☾ ● ☽ ○ ☾ ● ☽ ○ ☾ ● ☽ ○ ☾ ● ☽

Luxury feature/focal point: Turn your boring bed into a magical, "flying" slumber palace! Here's how:

Start by making a very elaborate and gothic but super-easy-to-make headboard:

1 Move your bed into a central-ish place in your bedroom, but with the head of the bed pushed up against a wall (preferably one that's painted purple).

2 Using easy-to-erase chalk and a ruler, draw a line on the wall where the top of the mattress lies.

3 Move the bed out of the way, and cover up all surfaces to protect them from the messy painting that's about to happen!

4 Still using the chalk, draw a headboard, using your original chalk line as the "base." Try fancy scrollwork like this one.

5 Now use paint to fill in your headboard outline. Black paint will give it an Old World wrought-iron look; or use a light color, like gold, if you want it to stand out more.

And now for the "flying" part:

1 Buy or make a bed skirt from see-through material (netting is fine) and put it around your bed so that it falls from the bottom of your mattress to the floor. (The easiest way to make a bed skirt is to get a large piece of material and lay it squarely over your bed base, then put your mattress back on top. For an average-sized single bed, your material should be approximately 2 yards (1.8 m) wide and 2-3/4 yards (2.5 m) long — which allows for a drop of about 15-1/2 inches (40 cm) for the "skirt" part.)

2 Put string lights under the skirt around your bed. The netting makes the lights fuzzy and spooky — as if your bed is hovering above the ground!

Added extras: Use things like fake spiders, owls, mice, and cobwebs left over from Halloween, and old colored bottles, candles, and candleholders to give an even spookier feel to your room.

Princess's parent persuader No. 4

YOU WANT: fancy effects – a canopy bed, mural of stars, bejeweled mirror, etc.

THE PARENTS WANT: to keep things straight and simple.

TYPICAL PARENT QUOTE: "You're not putting all that junk in your room!"

MINI POINT: Show them how great these things can look, with pictures cut out of magazines or printed from the Internet.

MAJOR POINT: Ask them to help you with your fancy effects (e.g., "But you're so very good at sewing," etc.). They'll end up being proud of the "junk" they've helped you make! (Even if they weren't fooled by your flattery for one second....)

Bubble's amazing Amazon

❝Because I have to share my room with my little sis, we're always arguing about what our room should look like. She likes cute fluffy animals, whereas I like to think about wild, exotic places and saving the planet! Anyway, we decided to compromise by having a jungle theme that included all our favorite things.**❞**

Theme: Wild jungle

Best for: Small or shared rooms

Would appeal to: Frustrated Friends desperate for an end to the ongoing war with an annoying sibling and/or a very outgoing, spontaneous kind of Friend with "adventurous" tastes.

Color scheme: Oranges, greens, and animal-print patterns.

Special effects: Cover *everything* with animal-print fun fur (go for "tiger" rather than "cow," though!). For instance, make your own cushion covers (see page 79), or glue fun fur onto things like your wastebasket.

Luxury feature/focal point: Add a fringe of exotic jungle vines dangling down one wall and a cute treetop canopy! Here's how to do it:

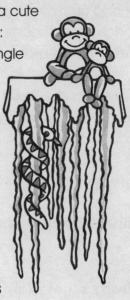

1 Paint one wall an intense jungle green.

2 Ask Dad or Mom to help you put up a row of shelves near the top of the wall.

3 To make your vines, cut about twenty 2-inch by 60-inch (5-cm x 152-cm) lengths of green felt (although you could use other material or some strong string instead).

4 Secure your vines with thumbtacks along the underside of your shelf.

5 Cover your shelves with green felt (or other material) so that it flops over the edge of your shelves and the tops of your vines, and tack it down with thumbtacks.

Ta-daaa! A comfy treetop canopy for all your (or your sis's) stuffed toys to romp around on!

(Tip: I also got a few of my sis's cuddly monkeys, spiders, snakes, etc., and tied them at various heights onto the vines. Even I'll admit they look cute!)

Added extra: Show you care about conservation by pinning up a map with the world's diminishing jungles and endangered species highlighted. (Check out the World Wildlife Fund Internet site for more information.)

That's it for the dreamiest of the dreamy bedrooms, BFs. Now how about doing three new looks on no (or very little) money? Take it away, girls!

★ ★ ★ ★ ★ ★ ★ ★ ★ ★ ★ ★ ★ ★ ★ ★ ★ ★

Three cheap 'n' easy radical re-dos

Missy's chillin'
Oriental chamber 自由

“I like this look because it looks very modern, neat, clean, and bright. To get it right, just think about keeping things simple and using loads of natural stuff, like plain fabrics, wood, and stone.**”**

Preparation: Clear out all your clutter (see Flower's feng shui tips on page 63).

Bed: For that Japanese-style low bed look, see if your parents will let you take off the legs of your bed (if it's got 'em!) or for an even lower bed, see if they'll remove the base unit and let you just have the mattress on the floor!

Color scheme: Keep the color theme as simple as you can: no patterned stuff — just blocks of neutral tones, like cream, beige, white, and black.

Windows: To give your room a bright hazy glow, make some beautifully simple Japanese-style curtains: Get two pieces of cheap white muslin (each one should be half the width of your window but twice as long). Then put one end of each "curtain" over a curtain rod and gently pull it down so that it is evenly doubled over. Do the same with the other curtain. Alter the mood of your room with different-colored muslin.

Lights: Get one of those huge, round paper lamp shades for your overhead light.

Walls: Chinese and Japanese writing looks really cool and arty — either stencil them on your walls (if you're allowed to) or copy the ones printed here, using black paint. Copy them on two white sheets of paper, put them into clip-frames and hang them around your room.

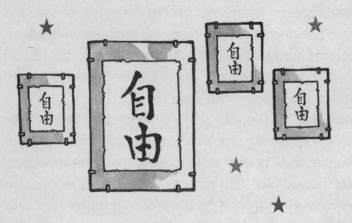

Accessories: Collect lots of natural objects, like twigs, stones, and shells, and display them simply around your room — long twigs look groovy in a big vase. Also, has Mom got a couple of houseplants you can borrow? (Palms and cacti are easy to look after and are very stylish!)

Flower's hippie hangout

"Creating the hippie look is really simple. I came up with this idea by copying the best parts from our house! The look basically has a retro 1960s feel to it and involves lots of things having to do with caring about the environment, peace, love, and "flower power." You'll like this best if you're naturally laid-back, just a little unconventional, and enjoy cozy, welcoming spaces!**"**

Preparation: Think peaceful thoughts to get in the right groove!

Bed: Cover your bed with a homey patchwork quilt or flowery bedspread. If you haven't got anything suitable, try tie-dyeing a sheet (see page 91) to go over your bed.

Color scheme: Go for pale purples and calming greens. If you want to add splashes of pattern, use a wild mix of lots of bright colors.

Windows: String some brightly colored plastic beads or crystals on various lengths of nylon thread (with knots at the end) and hang your bejeweled beauties from the top of your window, using a thumbtack, so they dangle in front of the windowpane. During the day your beauties will catch the sun and send shimmers of colored light around your room.

Walls: Make some cool wall hangings by getting a huge piece of plain cloth (muslin is cheap and looks nice and floaty) and painting designs on it with fabric paint. Try painting on huge flowers, the peace sign, or a slogan about something you feel strongly about (e.g.: Stop cruelty to animals now!) to go with your hippie theme; or you could tie-dye your wall hangings.

Furniture: Get that laid-back hippie vibe by putting down a few big, comfy floor cushions so you and your friends can sit around and just chill and chat (see page 79 for how to make floor cushions).

Accessories: A wind chime near your door will give a mystical jingle when your door is opened or closed. If your budget won't stretch to include a chime, then scented candles and incense will add to the mellow mood.

Princess's angelic slumber palace

❝This is my sophisticated version of a theme that uses lots of images of angels, stars, and clouds. It should make you feel as though you've walked into a little bit of heaven!**❞**

Preparation: Clean your room thoroughly — dust, smelly socks, and sticky fizzy drink stains are not what you expect to find in paradise.

Bed: To make your bed seem like it's floating among the clouds, make it into a fluffy heap with as many cushions and pillows (preferably with white covers) as you can find in the house. Then make a white muslin bed canopy and decorate it with angels and stars — I like gold fabric paint, but use whatever you can get. (See page 73 for Bubble's stencil tips, page 87 for how to make a bed canopy, and page 79 for cushion-making.)

Color scheme: Sky-blue and fluffy cloud-white, of course! Plus lots of gold-colored accessories.

Lights: A huge, white paper lantern overhead will give a nice, clear white light.

Walls: A fabulous idea is to write a word like "dream" or "angel" in as many different languages as you can find (try searching on the Internet; www.free-translator.com is a good site!) all over your walls.

Use a small paintbrush and your fanciest handwriting. It looks really arty if you use the same color as the paint on your walls, but just a shade or two lighter or darker.

Ceiling: Stick up loads of self-adhesive glow-in-the-dark stars, or paint stars and moons, using any spare paint you've got.

Accessories: Get as many angel-themed things as you can find. Plaster-cast cherubs spray-painted gold look wonderful! If you have, like, *no* money, rummage in the holiday decorations and see what suitable stuff you can find.

The great thing about these quick-fix ideas is that they are so easy, cheap, and versatile, you could change the look of your room almost as often as Princess does if you wanted to!

❝I'll have you know that I've actually had the angelic look for three whole months! I can't wait to create my next theme, though!**❞**

How about you, Friend? Got your creative vision yet? Figured out your schedule? Sketched your blueprint? Don't worry if you haven't. We Best Friends still have loads more ideas and magical makeover tips for you — and we're not going anywhere until you get it together!

And if you never get it together? Well, I suppose you could always let YOUR MOTHER DESIGN YOUR BEDROOM!!!

Ha! Not really. I just said that so you'd realize what's at stake here! COME ON!

★ ★
★

★ Making the Most of ★ What You've Got ★

So, Friend, do you want a mind-blowing, awesome bedroom but are up against an empty purse, parent power, or lack of time? Or do you simply feel uninspired by your small room? Have no fear, Friend, because we're here to look at some simple ways of turning your drab room into a fab pad!

66My big problem is keeping my room neat. My little sis is *the* messiest kid, and let's just say housework doesn't come naturally to me!**99**

66That's because you've not been following the teachings of feng shui (pronounced: fung shway).**99**

66Who's he, then, the new art teacher at school?**99**

66No, silly! It's an ancient Chinese philosophy that teaches you how to live in harmony with your environment.**99**

66Uh-oh, I feel a lesson in feng shui coming on!**99**

A quick lesson in feng shui

★ Feng shui is spookily old — dating back to China about 5,000 years ago.

★ It means wind and water, because that's what people had to be aware of when they built their homes (e.g., not to build where it's too windy or likely to flood).

★ The basic principle of feng shui is that your surroundings affect how you feel. In other words, messy, smelly, poorly designed living spaces don't make you a happy puppy!

★ An example of feng shui at work in your bedroom would be to use a vibrant color like orange around your desk to help you find the brainpower to do your homework, and a soft relaxing color like blue around your bed to help soothe you to sleep.

★ In feng shui, there are lots of odd rules based on old superstitions about how rooms and houses should be laid out. But behind the superstitions, you can actually find a lot of great modern design tips. Like these:

Rule 1: Don't position your bed so your feet point directly toward the door.

Superstition: This is known as the "death position" in China, because dead people are always carried out feet first — it's therefore considered to be bad luck.

Design tip: Opening the door and seeing a bed in a straight line in front of you is pretty boring (and a little drafty!). Try to create more interesting angles for your bed when you plan the layout of your room.

Rule 2: Never place your desk so that your back is to the door.

Superstition: Sitting with your back to the door makes you open to attacks from "backstabbers."

Design tip: It will make your work area seem less cramped if you sit with a wall behind you and face out into your room. Also, being able to see your door from your desk will mean The Parents can't catch you in the act of *not* doing your homework!

❝Now then, Bubble, let me tell you and our Friend how feng shui can help you tidy up a messy room.

❝One of the ideas of feng shui is that everything should have a home, and that if your space is a mess, you won't be able to find anything, you'll get frustrated, and your *ch'i* (Chinese for your inner energy) will be pooped!❞

Six steps to decluttering your bedroom by Flower (and her pal feng shui!)

1 Get three trash bags: one for junk to throw away; one for stuff to give to charity; and one for stuff that needs to find a place of its very own in your room.

2 Sort through all your stuff, asking yourself three questions:

a) Do I love it?

b) Do I really need it?

c) Is it useful?

Anything that gets "not really" twice should be trashed — unless you think it might be useful to someone else, then give it to charity.

3 If you haven't used something for more than two years — face it, you don't need it! Get rid of it now!

4 Keep the mess under control by having a mini clean-up every day (putting away clothes, homework, etc.). Promise yourself to do five minutes' worth every night before bedtime.

5 Keep your work space and makeup table clear of stuff that you don't use on at least a weekly basis.

6 Give each possession a definite home; even if it's under your bed, as long as it's organized and dust-free, that's fine!

Hey, Friend! Now you've turned your pigsty into a, uhm, sty-lish pad, want to know the secret of keeping it that way forever with very little effort?!? Well, according to Missy, it's all about storage....

Store and stash with Missy!

Shelve it

☺ Get dad to build loads of shelves!

☺ Put stuff you use a lot on the lower shelves so you can reach it easily, and stash stuff you don't use so much up top.

Box it

☺ Keep your stuff stashed in clear plastic boxes or wire trays (so you can see what's in 'em) and it keeps everything neat on the shelves and easier to move stuff up and down.

☺ Boxes can be stored in other nifty places — like under the bed.

Tag it

☺ Put big labels on all your drawers, files, and boxes — it'll help you find things when you need them.

File it

☺ If you have loads of paper — homework, letters, doodles, etc. — organize a filing system. I got an old filing cabinet from my mom's office and put a bunch of hanging files in it in ABC order — it cleaned up my room, no probs.

☺ If you have a copy of something on your computer, throw away the paper version — it isn't necessary in this day and age! (Always back up your files, though, in case your computer crashes!)

Stow it

☺ If you have a small room, put away everything you don't need until you do — e.g., bag your winter clothes in summer and put them in the attic for a few months.

Other tips

☺ Shoe racks that hang on a door or closet rod keep messes off the floor.

☺ Hooks on the backs of doors give you extra hanging space.

☺ Don't forget to use the "dead" space under beds and on tops of armoires.

Now that groovy Missy's got us in the mood, do any of you other Friends have some cheapo ways of adding *boom!* to your bedroom?

❝Accessories! Those little things that you don't actually *need* but that can make your room great and that you enjoy having around! Here's my essential guide....❞

Princess's necessary accessories (for a better bedroom!)

Beads Add instant glamour by trimming lamps, curtains, cushions, and whatever else you can think of with dangly trinkets.

Cushions Give your room a soft romantic look, and provide plenty of comfy sitting choices for visiting friends, with as many cushions of different shapes, sizes, and materials as you can find (see page 79 for cushion-making).

Feathers A touch of plumage is an inexpensive way to make your room look fabulously arty. Drape feather boas around mirrors and picture frames, and stick feathers instead of flowers into a vase — *et voila, tres glam, mes amis!*

Glitter Is something in your room looking sad, saggy, and sort of dull? "Glitterate" it! I can't think of much in this world that wouldn't look better with a coating of glitter paint lovingly smoothed on it.

Night skies Stick glow-in-the-dark stars on your ceiling, then lie back and visit a different universe.

Incense sticks Perfect for that new-age vibe! And you don't even need to burn them to catch a whiff of their exotic scent.

Knickknacks I like old perfume bottles; Molly has a thing for the stupidest joke products she can find; Bubble collects baseball player's autographs and photos (and has devoted a whole wall of her room to her fave team); Flower's room glistens with new-age crystals (some say they're a source of healing power). And Missy is wild about sunglasses (she currently owns thirteen pairs of shades!) Whatever you're into, display it proudly in your room. It's what makes you uniquely *you*.

Lights You can go from a cozy glowing hangout to a dazzling bright beauty salon with the flick of a switch. See if your mom's got a couple of old lamps you can jazz up, then try them in different places in your room to get the mood you want. For a magical touch, you can drape string lights around your room. Colored lightbulbs can create a chilled-out glow, and a mirror ball will give you an instant party atmosphere.

Mirrors Not only do mirrors make your room look bigger, but you get to catch glimpses of your beautiful self all the time! You can also use mirrors to reflect light around your room.

Posters OK, so putting up posters in your room is not an earth-shattering idea, but how about getting creative with your poster displays, huh?!? My three best ideas for groovy posters:

1 Be wacky: put your posters on the ceiling! Lie back on your bed and enjoy!

2 Be cool: place your posters so they make a checker-board design over one wall.

3 Be arty: instead of putting up ready-made posters, cut around your favorite athlete/pop star/kitten — their lifelike shape will really make them stand out and add depth to your room (as we designer types like to say).

Rugs Are you bored with staring at the same old floor? Add a fresh look with a brightly colored rug!

Smells Want to make your friends think they've just stepped into an exotic Eastern palace? Then stock up on potpourri, scented candles, incense sticks, and essential oils. They won't notice your room's a mess, just the gorgeous aromas!

WATCH IT, Friend!

Burning incense, candles, and essential oils can be a fire risk! Always ask Mom or Dad if you can use them, never leave anything that is burning unattended, and make sure you *always* extinguish them properly.

That sure is some awesome accessorizing, Princess!

❝Thanks, Molly, I guess all I'm telling our Friend is that she should have fun, be herself, and surround herself with lovely things!❞

Hey, now that P's finished, isn't it time for my two cents?

Okey-dokey, Bubs! And now, proving she is handier than a handyman with a set of extra hands, it's the moment we've all been waiting for...Ms. Handy-dandy herself, the one and only Bubble! (Loud applause and cheering!)

I may not be the neatest of the Friends or a trendy designer type like Princess, but because my parents are obsessed by 'economizing' (yawnsville!) and my dad's a do-it-yourself nut, I've become something of a Handy Makeover Queen.

Brighten up that junk (with Bubble!)

To begin touching up your old stuff and adding some magical touches to your room, all you need are some basic tools. See what you can piece together from my list, then let your imagination go wild!

Useful supplies for beginner junk brighteners

Brushes, rollers, sponges, etc. Experiment with different ways of applying paint to get different effects and finishes.

Day-Glo paint Ideal for creating glimmering stars and moons.

Double-sided tape Great for when glue isn't fast enough!

Dye A messy but fantastic way of giving old bedding and curtains a new look. It's probably best to get your mom involved in this one, because if she's anything like mine, she'll go ballistic if she catches you slopping around buckets of fuchsia dye. (See page 92 for more tips.)

Fun fur Adds comfort, style, and trendiness to any surface!

Gemstones Glue plastic ones on everything from mirrors to chair backs!

Glue gun A must for sticking things to things!

Glitter Makes the world a happier place!

Knobs Give a yucky dresser, chest of drawers, or even your bedroom door a totally radical new image simply by replacing the handles.

Metallic felt-tips Great for drawing fancy patterns onto stuff.

Muslin (or any floaty material) Perfect for making inexpensive curtains and fancy bed canopies.

Paint Can't afford a big can? No leftovers? Buy the smallest cans to be had and use them to paint borders or murals or on woodwork and doors. Special paints are great. My current favorites are denim finish, glitter paint, gold and silver metallic paints, and hot pink in gloss finish. Check your local do-it-yourself store for inspiration.

Ribbon Fem stuff up with bows.

Silk flowers Pretend you live in a sunny meadow and stick 'em over your walls, drawers, or wastebasket!

Stencils One of the grooviest tools in the junk brightener's box of tricks! Use stencils to paint themes and patterns (people, flowers, angels, animals, etc.) onto your stuff — including using them with fabric paints on your cushions, bedspread, and curtains.

Tassels Use big chunky ones in place of drawer knobs or use them as classy curtain tiebacks!

Trimmings Get out the glue gun and add velvet, fringe, beads, and braiding to *everything*!

Velcro Can't be bothered sewing? Stick this on with fabric glue, or get no-sew, iron-on hems.

"Got your kit together? Feel like testing out your junk-brightening skills? C'mon, Friend, and join one of my famous do-it-yourself projects!**"**

★ ★

Bubble's two favorite thrifty makeover projects

Project 1: Jazzing up an old wooden chair
What you need:

★ Paint (gloss is best) ★ Brushes ★ Old newspaper ★ Sandpaper (maybe) ★ Oh, and an old chair!

What you do:

Ask your parents for any leftover paint, then stand your chair on plenty of newspaper (to stop the dreaded drips!) and paint as much of it as you can see. Wait for the paint to dry (a couple of hours or so), then turn the chair over and paint the other side. (If you're painting a varnished surface, you may need to sandpaper it first; otherwise, the new paint won't stay on.)

Other tips: Use your imagination to add personal touches to your remade chair. How about sticking buttons or gemstones around the edges (not on the seat, though — ouch!), painting your name on the back, stenciling the chair with hearts, or painting parts of it different colors for a rainbow effect?

❝If you have furniture that doesn't match, you can paint it all the same color so it looks like a set. White gloss is boss because it's clean, bright, modern, and goes with everything.**❞**

Princess's Parent Persuader No. 5

YOU WANT: your bedroom to be a parent-free zone while you and your friends do all the painting and decorating yourselves.

THE PARENTS WANT: to be in charge of everything.

TYPICAL PARENT QUOTE: "No, you'll only make a mess."

MINI POINT: Ask them to start you off by showing you how it's done. Then ask them to let you take over, and maybe arrange for them to check your progress once an hour.

MAJOR POINT: Announce your intention to become an interior designer when you're older. Then say you fear that unless you are given this opportunity to explore your ambitions, the fire that burns within your soul will be smothered forever.

Project 2: Beautifying a boring tabletop or desktop with knickknacks and glitter.

What you need:

★ Paintbrush ★ Clear, quick-drying varnish ★ Glitter or glitter paint ★ Interesting knickknacks you want to immortalize on your tabletop. Pick things that will lie flat, like photos, confetti, pressed leaves or flowers, cutouts of angels, stars — or whatever else goes with your room's theme.

What you do:

Make sure the tabletop is clean and dry, then paint it with the glitter paint, if you have it. Or you can brush on a layer of varnish and sprinkle it with some glitter. Next, carefully brush the backs of your knickknacks with varnish and lay them down flat on the table (they must be almost completely flat!). Once everything is in place, gently give your top a few more coatings of varnish. Leave each coat to dry for about 30 minutes, or according to the instructions on the label, before putting on the next layer. It will need about five coats in all.

Other tips: Now that you've got the tabletop looking great, what about painting the legs with glitter paint or gluing on plastic gemstones, seashells, or even plastic spiders!

❝I've got loads of baseball stuff varnished onto mine — including photos of all the players from my fave team and a ticket stub from when Dad took me to see 'em. It looks top-notch!❞

Feel inspired by Bubble's super-artsy-craftsy creativity? Want to add some very special features to your room? Look no further than our next fascinating chapter, Friend, where we will explore some splendiferous items to make. Onward!

★ Stuff to Make ★

Unless your parents are, like, trazillionaires and have hired you a small army of interior designers, there comes a time in every Friend's makeover when she will have to get seriously practical. So if you want to know how to do everything from making a cushion to painting a mural, read on! (Unless, that is, you actually WANT YOUR DAD TO GO GET HIS HANDYMAN MANUAL.... Ha! I thought that would get you into gear!)

Flower's Foolishly easy-to-make Cushions ★

66Cushions are a simple way of making your room look inviting. Here are my basic cushion-making instructions — use them to make anything from pretty mini cushions to humongous floor cushions! And don't worry, you don't need to be a superseamstress to make them!**99**

What you need:

★ Material (Fun fur is easy to work with, and it's cheap and looks gorgeous. Or maybe you've got some old clothes you can cut up and use?) ★ Stuffing (for this, you could use an old cushion, foam pad, soft-toy stuffing, old clothes, tights, etc., or polystyrene balls.) ★ Thread ★ Needle (longer, sturdier ones are sometimes easier to work with) ★ Pins ★ Scissors ★ Velcro or snap fasteners (optional)

What you do:

1 Decide what size you want your cushion to be. If you are using a loose filling, this can be pretty flexible — but a 14 inch by 14 inch (36-cm x 36-cm) shape will give you a nice medium-sized cushion. If you are making a case for a foam pad or old cushion, you will need to measure it and add 3/4 inch (1.5 cm) on each side to allow for the seams.

2 Cut out one cushion front and one back from your material, according to your chosen measurements.

3 Place the two pieces of material with the right sides facing together (i.e., so the patterned sides are not showing), and pin it all the way around — this will keep the material in place. Then sew around three sides about 3/4 inch (1.5 cm) from the edge, leaving the final fourth side open.

4 Remove the pins and turn the cover right side out. Insert your stuffing, then turn under the edges of the opening by about 3/4 inch (1.5 cm). Now sew the Velcro or snaps into place on the inside edge of the opening, or stitch it closed.

5 Lie back on your lovely new cushion — you've earned a rest!

Special note: If you are using loose filling, like polystyrene balls, and want to be able to wash your cushion cover, it will be easier if you put your filling into an inner cushion case first. You can make it exactly as above, only slightly smaller (about a half inch less on all sides), using unwanted scraps of material and then stitching it closed.

★

The BFs' secret-stash stowaway cushion!

One of the great things about making your own cushions is that you can create the perfect hiding place for keeping precious private items (like your diary) away from the prying eyes of siblings!

What you need:

★ Two cushion covers, each with one side left open (one cover should be slightly smaller than the other — only the bigger one needs to be nice fabric.)

★ Loose filling or two foam pads

★ Velcro or snap fastenings

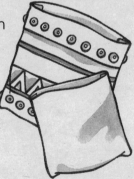

What you do:

1 Fold the opening on each cover inward so that it has a hem of 1 inch (3 cm) all the way around. Attach the Velcro (using fabric glue) or sew the snaps to the inner edges of the opening — so that when your cushion is closed, everything is concealed and the sides all look the same.

2 Stuff the smaller cover with your filling and insert your secret stash in the middle. (If you're using the foam pads, they'll act like a sandwich kind of thing.) Then close your cushion.

3 Insert the smaller inner cushion upside down (so that its opening is on the opposite side to the second opening) into the slightly bigger outer cushion and close that, too.

How it works: The stowaway cushion looks normal, but even if a snooper starts messing with it, the fastenings should put them off. However, if you have supersnoopers around, you should slip a "guilty-reader note" inside the first cover. It could read something like this:

Dear Supersnooper,
Please immediately halt your snooping! If you go any further you will unearth my diary's hiding place. I've hidden it here for a reason, because it contains my private thoughts and feelings — if I'd meant for you to see them I wouldn't have hidden them. Please respect my rights as a human being. If you want to know something about me, you can always try talking to me.
Be warned: no good will come of further snooping.
Love, peace, and harmony,

_____ (your name here)

"There's nothing as annoying as someone getting hold of your stuff. I should know. Nothing I own is safe from the sticky fingers of my little sis.... That is, until I made myself a pair of pocket curtains — they're curtains but they have loads of pockets all over them! It took ages for Sticky Fingers to realize I was hiding things in my 'pockets'; and now, to be safe, I switch things around constantly or use the ones higher up.**"**

Bubble's (semi-secret) pocket curtains

What you need:

★ Curtains (solid colored ones look better because they show off the pockets, but you could use any) ★ A bunch of old scarves, bandanas, napkins, or back pockets ripped from seat of old jeans ★ Pins ★ Needle ★ Thread

What you do:

1 Turn each scarf (etc.) into pockets of various shapes and sizes by either folding in half diagonally — so you have a triangular shape with one corner facing directly down — or folding in half to give you a rectangular shape.

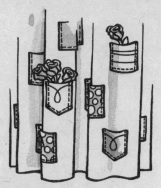

2 Lay the curtains flat and pin on your pockets, either in rows or randomly.

3 Now sew the pockets onto the curtains, leaving the top of each pocket open, and remove the pins as you go.

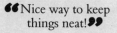

66Nice way to keep things neat!99

66You could have some silk flowers peeking out of each pocket for a hippie touch!99

Wow, we're really getting going with the nifty ideas. Princess, how about you?

66Well, of course, being the most *princessy* of us all, I think I should probably be the one to tell our Friend how to make her bed look fit for royalty. Friends, be prepared to be the envy of girls everywhere as you learn to make:99

Classic canopies and floaty four-posters

66Use a simple canopy to highlight your bed, or go for all-out fantasy with the surprisingly easy-to-make four-poster.99

WATCH IT, Friend! Since this involves the tricky feat of screwing things into ceilings, you should ask one of your parents for help. (We know you want to do it yourself, but give your parents a break — after all, they like to feel needed, too.)

For a basic canopy, you need:

★ Lightweight floaty material (like muslin, netting, or something silky; and preferably one that doesn't fray or run — so you don't have to sew lots of boring hems)

★ 60 inch (160 cm) length of fishing line (also called monofilament)

★ Four biggish screw eyes (these have the bodies of screws, but instead of having flat heads, they have a loop that's used to hold wire or thread)

What you do:

1 Cut your material to the size you need. (For a single bed, your canopy should be slightly wider and longer than your bed — approximately 49 inches by 92 inches; 125 cm x 235 cm.)

2 Attach a 15 inch (40 cm) length of the fishing line onto each corner of the canopy by sewing it on with a large-eyed darning needle — make about seven secure stitches, then leave the end dangling.

3 Ask a parent to put screws into the ceiling above your bed. They should be spaced apart to the exact measurements of your canopy.

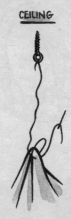

CEILING

4 Get a parent's help to tie the dangly ends of the fishing line securely to the screw eyes in the ceiling. Your canopy should now look as though it's hovering above your bed!

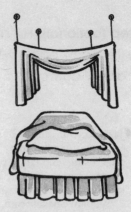

To make the four-poster version, you also need:

★ Four lengths of your material (approximately 8 inches by 3 yards; 20 cm x 2.65 m) for the corner drop panels

What you do:

Follow 1 as above

2 Use fabric glue or sew each of the drop panels onto the canopy top. Make sure the top of each drop panel fits squarely around each corner of the canopy top.

Follow 2, 3, and 4 above

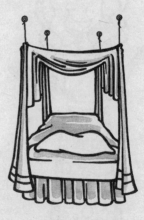

Then gasp and gape as you behold your four lovely drop panels cascading beautifully to the floor!

Last step (optional): For an extra added touch, tie each panel with a ribbon or scarf halfway down.

66 Jazz up your canopy by painting on a design of your choice. Try doing stars, using gold fabric paint, or a quote written in fancy lettering ("sleep perchance to dream" from William Shakespeare, for example). 99

66 Don't forget you could give your canopy a crazy dose of color by tie-dyeing it! Anything that stays still for more than five minutes in our house gets shoved into the tie-dye bucket. We're crazy about it! It's a great way to turn dull things into multicolored masterpieces! Here's how we do it: 99

How to tie-dye with Flower power!

What you need:

★ The item to be dyed (old cotton sheets and pillowcases are perfect) ★ Dye ★ Rubber gloves ★ Rubber bands ★ Salt ★ Two old buckets or bowls ★ Cold water

What you do:

1 Start by pinching pieces of the material into cone shapes and tightly wrapping them with the rubber bands. This gives you swirly circular patterns when you're finished — the bigger the cone, the bigger the circle will be.

2 Following the manufacturer's instructions on the package, carefully mix the dye with water in the bowl or bucket.

3 Sprinkle a few teaspoons of salt into the dye mixture — this will help set the pigment in the dye.

4 Then, wearing your rubber gloves to keep your hands from

staining, carefully dip your item into the dye and leave it to soak for about an hour.

5 Carefully remove your item from the dye and put it into an old bowl; let it sit and dry for about three to four hours. Then rinse thoroughly with water and remove the rubber bands. Hey, presto, groovy bedding/wall-hanging/curtains *and* a piece of original artwork made by you!

WATCH IT, Friend! Dyeing can be a messy business. Always make sure you've protected all surfaces with heaps of newspapers, and wear old clothes. And ask The Parents' permission before you turn your house into a rainbow land of splishy-splashy beauty (they might not see it that way).

Speaking of rainbows and splishy-splashy effects reminds me of Bubble with a paintbrush!

"OK, so I may be a little messy, but that's the price you pay for creativity! I'm sure I could show our Friend some interesting paint effects for her walls.**"**

Splish-splash: a lesson in paint effects by Ms. Bubble

66Nothing transforms a room quite as dramatically as painting it. Here, I've picked out the most dramatic techniques I know of for painting your walls.**99**

Candy-stripe walls

You can do this on just one wall or a small area. If you're after a classy look, use subtle shades; if you want a jazzier effect, use bolder, contrasting colors. Guess which one I like best?!

What you need:

★ Two shades of paint ★ Painter's tape ★ Plumb line (You'll probably have to ask a parent to help you on this one.) ★ Small paintbrush

What you do:

1 Paint your wall with one of the colors and let it dry (keeping in mind that some paints might need a second coat).

2 Mark off your stripes by blocking out every other 6 inch (15 cm) vertical section, using the tape. The plumb line (basically a string with a weight at the bottom) will help you keep your tape straight because when you hold it at the top of the wall, the weight at the bottom keeps the string taut and exactly straight.

3 Carefully paint the exposed area of wall with your second color, leave to dry, then remove tape (it's designed not to rip paint off walls).

WATCH IT, Friend!

Make less mess by putting loads of newspaper or old sheets over *everything* not to be painted, before you start. Mark off the surface to be painted, using painter's tape to keep paint from splashing into adjoining areas. And make sure the room is ventilated, or the fumes will get you!

★ * ★ * ★ * ★ * ★ * ★ * ★ * ★ * ★ * ★ ★ *

Murals

Even if you think you have, like, zero artistic skills, painting an effective mural can be surprisingly easy. Try these two:

Tropical scene mural
What you need:
★ Mini cans of paint (in brown, green, yellow, and blue) ★ Paintbrush
What you do:
1 For the sand, paint some yellow on the bottom of your

wall. (You could even add a small amount of real sand to the paint for a genuine texture effect!)

2 Paint a long brown trunk coming out of the sand. Start the trunk broad at the bottom and taper it at the top.

3 Add a few spiky, green palm-type leaves. Simple, eh?

Mega-massive mural

The trouble with doing bigger, more ambitious murals is that it can be very hard to keep the proportions right when you draw things on a large scale — but not when you try this method!

What you need:

★ Pencil ★ Eraser ★ Sketch pad ★ Ruler ★ Measuring tape ★ Paint ★ Brushes and a big scoop of courage!

What you do:

1 Start by making a sketch of your design on paper.

Then draw a grid over your drawing, so you end up with, say, lots of 2-inch by 2-inch (5-cm x 5-cm) boxes.

2 Draw a corresponding grid in pencil on your wall but at four times the scale (with 8-inch by 8-inch; 20-cm x 20-cm boxes).

3 Now draw your design on the wall, being careful to copy into the larger boxes *only* what's in the smaller boxes on your sketch. Once you're happy with your drawing, you can start painting.

Best Friends TOP TIP

If you're not allowed to paint your walls, try decorating them with inspirational quotes! If you hear or read something brilliant, all you do is copy it out on a piece of paper (I like to do mine on the computer and use fancy lettering) and hang it where you can see it. My current inspirational quote is: "Don't let school interfere with your education!" (said by famous American author Mark Twain).

Well, BFs, I'm sure our Friend is suffering from information overload right about now! I think it's time to see what bothersome bedroom worries still remain unsolved in Friendsville. BFs, get your problem-solving advice ready!

Your bedroom-decorating Problems Solved

Can't decide between funky futuristic and junky retro? Having a hard time sharing your room with your pesky sis? Is living in a "shoe box" getting you down? We've been there! And now we're here to help you! Fire away, readers!

letter 1

Babyish room gloom

Dear Best Friends

The decor of my bedroom hasn't changed since I was six! Although I like pink, everything I've got is pink — including a stenciled-on border of pink baby rabbits. What's the easiest way of giving it an older look?

Ex bunny lover, 10, Cleveland

What the Best Friends say

 What about painting all your walls halfway up with a new color, leaving the pink on the top half! Now, that's cool!

 Then you could get a trendy wallpaper border to cover up your bunnies.

 Yeah, pick a border that matches the pink and your new color to tie it all in. I like pink and purple together, then maybe a pink, purple, and orange striped border.

▶

Limit the number of stuffed toys you have out — maybe keep your five faves, then store the rest away.

letter 2

Poster poser
Dear Best Friends
I would love to cover one of my walls with posters of my favorite band, but my mom and dad say I can't because posters will "ruin the walls." Please help. I can't stand my dull walls any longer!

Florence, 11, Chicago

What the Best Friends say

 Buy a packet of Sticky Tac, or something similar, then invite your parents to your room for a demonstration of its non-marking qualities! Also try offering them a guarantee, promising to repaint your walls if they do get damaged.

 Explain, with a slight pout, that they are suffocating your artistic spirit. Maybe they'll feel bad and say yes to the posters.

letter 3

Little room = big problem!
Dear Best Friends
Please help me. I have the smallest bedroom known to girlkind. Got any tips?

Billie Mae, 9, a tiny lair somewhere

What the Best Friends say

OK, Friend, anything to help. Here's a Decorating Tip especially for you!

▶

★ Decorating tip! ★

What to do if your room is small (besides cry and stamp your foot!)

★ Get lots of mirrors — they make a room look bigger and brighter.

★ Avoid patterns and dark colors — they'll make it seem cramped and "busy."

★ Go for light colors and leave your ceiling white (dark colors make ceilings appear lower, light colors appear to heighten them).

★ Avoid unnecessary furniture — for example, have shelves instead of bookcases.

★ Get rid of your clutter!

★ You could try making your bed look sofalike when you've got friends over. Simply push your bed lengthwise against a wall, remove your pillow, cover all of the bed with your bedspread or a quilt, and line up a row of pillows against the wall.

New curtains for certain!

Dear Best Friends

My room's done in a moon and stars theme and I've found this wonderful piece of material with all the signs of the zodiac on it that I'm dying to have as new curtains for my room. The trouble is, I don't have a clue how to make curtains, I can't sew, and my mom says she hasn't got time to make some. Any ideas?

Kelly, 11, New York City

What the Best Friends say

You can make curtains out of anything without having to sew! Try pinning the material straight onto the top of the window frame — and use a scarf or ribbon tied around the middle of the material when you want to let some light in! Better ask The Parents' permission before you do this one, though.

Or for an instant "real" curtain, you could turn over a hem of about 6 inches (15 cm) at the top of your material and hold it down with some of that no-sew iron-on hem stuff. This would leave you a channel all along the top of your curtains that you could put a curtain rod through — which could then be hung normally. You might want to use iron-on hems for the sides and bottoms of your curtains to prevent fraying.

Bedroom-sharing horror!

Dear Best Friends

My seven-year-old sister Daisy had to move into my room after my mom had our new baby brother a few months ago. I am in despair! What used to be my big, beautiful bedroom is now a pigsty of broken doll parts, teddy bears, and single socks, and just this week the wall sprouted a crop of Cinderella posters. Daisy is really beginning to annoy me — I have no privacy left. What can I do?

Kirsten, 10, Denver

What the Best Friends say

 What about poor Daisy?! She's used to being the youngest, now she's been "replaced" by a baby. She's totally lost her room, and to finish it all off, her big sister is annoyed with her! Try to find it in your heart to welcome her into your room.

 Yeah, well, that's OK for you to say, Flower. You don't have to put up with the hours of screechy, off-key recorder practice or the endless threats to "tell Mom on you" like me and Molly do.

I think you've got to gently set some limits. What about dividing the room in two and getting her to keep all her stuff in her half? Since you're the oldest and probably have more stuff, maybe you should try to get the bigger half! Color-coding would be a good way of marking where the room's divided; see if your parents will let you paint your half of the room a different color from Daisy's.

For privacy, you could have a four-poster canopy over your bed (see page 87), and maybe even have it curtained all the way around — then make it a rule that Daisy isn't allowed in your "tent"!

letter 6

Day-Glo no go, says Mom
Dear Best Friends
I really want to paint my walls bright orange, but my mom says absolutely no way. How can I persuade her to change her mind?

Ella, 9, Los Angeles

What the Best Friends say

It sounds like your mom is pretty unmovable on this one. How about picking out a slightly less intense orange that your mom wouldn't mind? Then decorate with loads of bright orange, pink, green, and yellow accessories — they'll offset the color on your walls and make your whole room more lively.

letter 7

Paper vs paint
Dear Best Friends
We've just moved into a new house and my parents say it's up to me whether my walls get paper or paint. What would the BFs do?

Ruby, 12, Seattle

What the Best Friends say

Paint's definitely trendier.

Absolutely paint, no contest! The thing with wallpaper is that once it's up, it's a real pain to take down again, so you'll probably have to keep it for years and years. Paint is much more flexible — you can do stencils, murals, and other touches, and scuffs and marks can be touched up easily.

Go for both! Paint your walls, then put up little wallpaper borders around the top or halfway up. You can get some designer-looking ones with trendy patterns, and they're easy to put up and take down.

My dull room horror

Dear Best Friends

Everything in my room is very plain;· I have a gray carpet, beige curtains, cream-colored walls, and a matching bedside table, dresser, and chest of drawers in a boring oak finish. What are the cheapest and easiest ways of livening up my dull room?

Lily, 11, Bleaksville

What the Best Friends say

 You're in need of some color — fast! First, buy a small can of paint, say in pink, and carefully paint pink squares of different sizes all over your walls. Next, buy some matching pink tissue paper, enough to cover your window. Then, cut out loads of different-sized square "peepholes" into the tissue paper. Make a cardboard frame the same size as the *inside* of your window frame and stick the tissue paper to it. Wedge the whole thing into the window frame. Finally, add a pink rug (shaggy bath mats look cute and are usually cheaper than ordinary rugs). Ta-daa! Within a few hours, your room will look very trendy and alive!

 I'd cover up some of that wood, too — a pretty scarf thrown over the bedside table would make all the difference.

You need to give your room something new every week — even a different screen saver on your computer or a new poster of your fave celeb — new stuff keeps it looking fresh!

Funky or junky?

Dear Best Friends

I'm about to completely redecorate my bedroom! The trouble is, I'm torn between two great themes: funky futuristic (lots of silver and plastic, and things with aliens) or junky 1970s retro (with lots of crazy patterns and a groovy orange and brown color scheme). What do you think?

Marina, 10, St. Louis

What the Best Friends say

 I think you should do the quiz in the next fab chapter!

103

The Quiz

This is the part where we find out exactly what bedroom theme would *really* suit your personality, just what your natural style truly is, and whether you're a Handy Annie or a Dotty Disaster of home improvement. Yes, Friends, it's the ultimate bedroom-based quiz....

R U a bedroom beauty or a bedroom bozo?

Check off one of the answers after each question, then turn to page 110, add up your scores, and find your profile. And please note, we only accept honest answers here, Friend!

1 Pick your favorite bedroom color scheme from the following:
a) Bright white with occasional glints of gold
b) Sumptuous feast of reds
c) Pale green and cotton-candy pink
d) Citrusy lemon with an eggplant purple contrast
e) Burnt orange rippled with azure blue
f) Oatmeal blended with beige blotches

2 Which of these "design features" would/does most make you cringe around your house?

a) Lace curtains — sooo frumpy!

b) Flowery furniture in the living room — enough said!

c) So-called "mood" lighting — what's that about?!

d) Brass pokers by the gas fireplace — they don't fool anyone!

e) Designer shoe trees — how fussy!

f) Reading matter in the toilet — yuck!

3 The last artsy-craftsy thing you did was (check off whichever is closest):

a) Helped Dad put up some shelves

b) Put some beads in my hair

c) Looked through one of Mom's interior design magazines

d) Jazzed up a couple of boxes to use as storage

e) Made a cotton-ball snowman when I was five

f) Customized a postcard to use as a bookmark (well, OK, I wrote my name on it in glitter pen!)

4 Which of the following places would you most like to visit?

a) Sunny California — You get to wear groovy bell bottoms and little crop-tops and ride around the awesome countryside on the back of a huge motorcycle, your long hair flowing in the warm breeze.

b) Africa on safari — Nothing could be better than camping out under the stars listening to the strange sounds of the sub-Saharan night.

c) Roswell, New Mexico — It's where all the space aliens land, apparently. Now that would be a great science project....

d) Rome — It's meant to be really chic and stylish, plus all that architecture and art must be so inspiring!

e) New York City — a totally cool city full of fascinating people. It would be so fantastic to just hang out people-watching at a sidewalk café.

f) The Great Barrier Reef in Australia — Snorkel in crystal clear water among the amazing coral and colorful fishes (avoiding the big ones with teeth, though!).

5 Which of these statements best describes your room?

a) Matching bedspread, curtains, and lamp shade (bought by Mom), muted color scheme

b) Cozy and welcoming, with lots of knickknacks and cute details

c) Very modern, with everything in its right place, bold and bright color scheme

d) Colorful and curious, with loads of quirky objects

e) Moody, packed with interesting textures, photos, and dim lighting

f) Stylish, with coordinated fabrics, fem touches, and a cool, light color scheme

6 Which of these statements most accurately reflects the condition of your bedroom? (Come on, be honest now — go take a quick look!)

a) OK, I admit it, I'm a neat freak — everything's very ordered; I even line up the stuff on my desk in order of size.

b) I don't see the point of making places look fancy — and you won't find lots of unnecessary possessions, either; just my books and bed kept in good order.

c) It smells lovely (I sprayed some air freshener around earlier) and my friends tell me it looks "casually elegant."

d) The floor is pretty much covered with my stuff and there's a dust ball bigger than the cat lurking under the bed.

e) Kind of messy, with piles of clothes and books here and there — and, oops, a couple of days' worth of cups that Mom keeps asking me to bring to the kitchen.

f) It's been a few days since it had a good cleaning, but I always keep things cleared away and the bed made.

7 How often would you say you experiment with a different personal look? (Pick nearest statement.)

a) My look is perfectly fine. I hate all that fashionable stuff — only the other day, the principal praised my no-nonsense outfit.

b) I love shopping for new clothes and shoes.

c) I like to mess around with hair accessories and little bits of makeup and nail polish.

d) I have two looks — daytime and nighttime!

e) I like to customize my clothes to my taste — I think I look unique (although Mom says "scruffy"!).

f) I always try on loads of outfits before I go out, and I just recently got a new hairstyle.

8 Your desk suddenly becomes wobbly; what do you do?

a) Get excited about my new "project" and ask Dad if I can borrow his saw.

b) Tell my parents I need a new desk.

c) Stick some cardboard under the weak leg to stop it from wobbling.

d) Ask a parent to fix it.

e) Do my homework sitting on my bed instead.

f) Keep meaning to look at it, then forget.

9 If you could become one of the following, which career would you choose?

a) Fitness guru to the famous

b) Pop star

c) Ecologist

d) Interior designer

e) Science teacher

f) Writer

10 Which of the following would you most like to have in your bedroom? (They all cost the same!)

a) A chic dresser in pale wood and shiny chrome

b) The latest high-tech music system

c) An amazing four-poster bed canopy made of Japanese silk

d) A laptop computer with Internet access

e) A platform bed — the kind with storage drawers below and a bookcase headboard

f) Double-glazed windows — allowing peace and quiet for doing homework

Now find out what kind of bedroom decorator you are!

Question 1	a = 1	b = 4	c = 3	d = 5	e = 2	f = 6
Question 2	a = 3	b = 1	c = 6	d = 2	e = 5	f = 4
Question 3	a = 5	b = 3	c = 1	d = 2	e = 6	f = 4
Question 4	a = 3	b = 5	c = 6	d = 1	e = 4	f = 2
Question 5	a = 6	b = 3	c = 2	d = 5	e = 4	f = 1
Question 6	a = 2	b = 6	c = 1	d = 5	e = 4	f = 3
Question 7	a = 10!	b = 2	c = 3	d = 5	e = 4	f = 1
Question 8	a = 5	b = 1	c = 2	d = 3	e = 6	f = 4
Question 9	a = 5	b = 2	c = 3	d = 1	e = 6	f = 4
Question 10	a = 1	b = 2	c = 3	d = 4	e = 5	f = 6

If you scored under 18 you are a Bedroom Beauty!

Ups: Wow, are you classy or what?! You instinctively know what's stylish and aren't afraid to experiment with adventurous new looks — you are a trendsetter and everyone secretly wants to be just like you.

Downs: You can be just a little snobbish about other people's tastes, and don't actually like do-it-yourself projects that much — after all, you might spoil your manicure!

You are most like: Princess

You should try: Princess's four-poster canopy (page 87)

If you scored 18–25 you are a Slumber-pad Perfectionist!

Ups: Can there be anybody cooler than you? We don't think so! You really enjoy experimenting with different looks, are amazingly organized and practical, and are fashion-aware without being faddish.

Downs: You can be overly efficient sometimes — old stuff can be put to good use, too, y'know. And when was the last time you hugged your teddy bear, huh? Whaddya mean, he's in storage?!

You are most like: Missy

You should try: Missy's cool storage ideas (page 64)

If you scored 26–33 you are a Cozy-den Darling!

Ups: You are a very spiritual, emotional kind of girl and really respect the environment (including your bedroom!), which is reflected in the tranquil vibes coming from you and your homey nest.

Downs: Sometimes your taste can get *too* fem and cute — you could try to be just a little more adventurous.

You are most like: Flower
You should try: refinishing an old tabletop (page 77)

If you scored 34–41 you are a Unique Groovy Stylist

Ups: You have a very individual sense of style — some would say kooky. Everybody loves coming to your place, not just because you are a great hostess but because every so often there's a new weird and wonderful creation to look at.

Downs: More neatness and less deep-thinking could see you reach Bedroom Beauty status — but then you wouldn't be lovely you!

You are most like: Molly

You should try: decluttering your room the feng shui way (page 60)

If you scored 42–50 you are a Bunk Punk!

Ups: Everybody thinks you haven't got a clue when it comes to style — but actually you've got the most style of us all! It's just that you are a deeply eccentric genius, and others are too conventional to see it! Plus, you are amazingly practical.

Downs: The chaos! The reason nobody understands your sensational style is because everyone is too horrified by the avalanche of muddy boots, dirty socks, books, paintings from when you were two, chocolate wrappers, stringless tennis rackets, and possibly a sleeping elephant or two, that greets them when your bedroom door is opened.

You are most like: Bubble

You should try: a mega mural (page 95)

If you scored over 50 you are a Bedroom Bozo!

Ups: You probably don't actually care that you're a bozo, because you really can't be bothered with anything as earthly as style!

Downs: You're missing out on the joy of color and other things of eye-pleasing loveliness!

You are most like: a bozo!

You should try: to get out more!

Almost good-bye!

Yes, it's getting near the time when we must leave you to continue your bedroom makeover by yourself! Sob! But before we go, it occurred to us Best Friends that there's a ton of other exciting themes we haven't even mentioned! So, lovers of prancing pink hippos, read on for more theme-related fun.

Other Room Makeovers

First of all, let me start this chapter with an apology:

Dear lovers of the prancing pink hippo theme,
I regret that, for reasons of good taste, we are unable to bring you coverage of this theme — there really is room only for the best themed-bedroom ideas in this book!
Love,
The Best Friends xxx

OK, Friends, let's go through our most brilliant theme ideas and our top tips to go with them!

The BFs top ten fave bedroom themes 'n' styles (in alphabetical order!)

1 American retro

Cool, clean 1950s look using lots of lime green and pale pink. Think old-fashioned jukeboxes, polka-dot prints, and Mickey Mouse posters.

 Thrifty TIP Save your old Coke bottles and display them in a line with a silk flower standing in each one.

 Flash TIP Do one wall using the candy-stripe painting method (described on page 93), in lime green and pale pink — it will look cool!

2 Arabian night-nights

Achieve this look with rich colors, exotic silky and satiny materials, and a floaty canopy bed (see page 87). Try to give your room a tentlike feel by putting up swaths of material draped artily around. Think big decorative tassels and gold-framed mirrors, and stick plastic gemstones everywhere.

Thrifty TIP

See if your mom's got any old party dresses in fab material that she'll let you cut up and use to make cushions — see how on page 79.

Flash TIP

Do a mural of a desert night sky on one wall! All you have to do is paint it a lovely dark midnight blue, then paint a huge bright full moon low on the horizon and as many twinkly stars as you like.

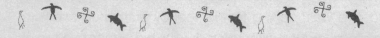

3 Fashion passion

Make your room a trendy hangout with loads of fashion-inspired stuff. Go for a "boutique" look with lots of mirrors and a makeup table packed with interesting hair accessories and things to mess around with, and hang large floppy hats and slogan T-shirts on coat hangers around your walls.

Thrifty TIP Put up lots of posters of fashion shoots cut from glossy magazines.

Flash TIP For the color scheme, go for bold, bright walls — one yellow, one orange, and one red — leaving the last one white. Hey, you might need it as background for a "photo shoot"!

4 Hawaiian holiday

Go on a tropical vacation every day with this look! Create your beach atmosphere by painting the bottom half of your walls in sand-colored textured paint and the top halves in sea blue, and add a palm mural. Accessorize with lots of exotic plastic flowers, cacti, etc., and it's "Aloha, baby!"

Make a collage of photos of you and your family on vacation — also ask your friends to contribute snapshots of themselves in beachwear!

Bamboo blinds would be marvelous!

❝You'd better take a look at my Parent Persuader on page 18 if you're after some of those, though!❞

5 Madame Mexico

Turn your dark room into a scene of sizzling spiciness, with a hot orange and intense red color scheme, then accessorize with chili string lights and green plastic cacti.

Thrifty TIP

Make a mini poncho for your teddy bear out of an old piece of material cut into an oblong shape. Make a slit in the middle for the head hole. Sooo cute!

Flash TIP

Paint "flames" along the bottom borders of your walls using upward "swooshes" of alternate yellow, orange, and red paint, then carefully outline them in black — hey, presto! A snazzy flame border!

6 Movie madness

Go for either a general glam celeb style or give your room a theme based on your favorite movie! Put film posters on your wall, and fill your room with star-shaped stuff.

For a laugh, make a shrine to your fave film star by making a stand-up silhouette of him or her. (Cut around a picture of your star from a magazine and mount it on cardboard.) Then stand the celeb on an altar (OK, your makeup table), surround it with candles, and present regular "offerings" — like a piece of your chocolate!

Stars' makeup tables always have lights around the mirrors — do the same with your bedroom mirror by stringing lights around the edges! Now you can see just how gorgeous you really are — you star of the future, you!

7 Pretty 'n' pink

Celebrate being a girl by turning your bedroom into a fem, fluffy pink nest! Soften the pink with lots of creamy colors, and use hearts and roses to add depth and delight!

Make your room smell pretty as well as look pretty with a bowl of rose or peach potpourri.

For ultimate fem lounging, get a chaise longue. (Y'know, one of those old-fashioned sofa things that looks like a cross between a mini bed and a reclining chair.) You can make your own version of one by getting a lawn lounger (if The Parents don't have one to lend you, maybe you could ask them for one?) and covering it with a 2-yard (2-m) length of glossy pink imitation satin and lots of matching cushions.

8 Super sci-fi

Midnight blue walls, gold stars, and arty murals (see page 94) of star-sign constellations would be a good start to this look. Then think spaceships, aliens, and any other futuristic stuff.

Thrifty TIP

Paint big almond-shaped alien eyes around your room in glow-in-the-dark paint — sp-sp-sp-spooky!

Flash TIP

Turn your bed into a hovering spaceship by copying the tips for the magical "flying" slumber palace from page 45, but give your bed a space-age headboard and a silvery-gray bedspread instead.

9 Two for one!

Can't decide between two themes? Have it all by using stuff from both — think futuristic witch or a hippie beach holiday! A good trick is to make your stuff reversible — or as much of it as you can!

Thrifty TIP
Make a two-themed cushion by having tiger-stripe fun fur on one side (jungle theme) and pink satin on the other (fem theme).

Flash TIP
Go totally wild and divide your room in two and have different themes on the two sides!

10 Urban honey

Get this look with minimum junk, modern furniture, graffiti doodles, and glossy ads of cool sneakers used as posters.

 Paint one wall with blackboard paint and stock up on chalk for doodle parties!

 Leave a skateboard lying casually around for instant street chic. Don't worry, you don't actually need to know how to ride it. Don't stand on it; sit on it and rock from side to side every now and then. People will think you're just a very modest, laid-back skate chick!

And now, it really is "good night" from us....

And so, with a big sad sigh, we Best Friends must say night-night and sweet bedroom dreams to you, our newest Friend... but only for now! Because we've got loads more to tell you about, some other time.

See you soon.

Big hugs, and let the bedroom bug bite!

Molly
x

Later, Missy ☺

Just remember, accessorize,
accessorize, accessorize!
Princess xx

Peace, love,
and a happy
space.
Flower xxxx

And, hey, hope your dream bedroom
comes true! Bubble! ooo